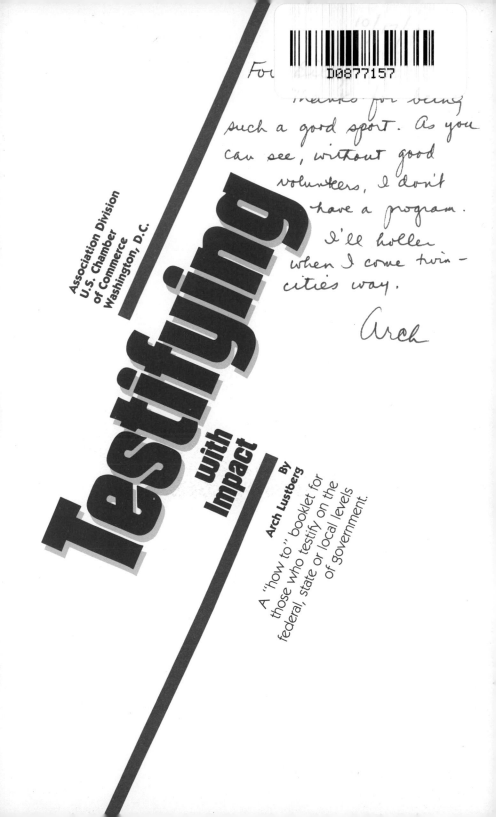

For ... Thanks for being such a good sport. As you can see, without good volunteers, I don't have a program. I'll holler when I come twin-cities way.

Arch

**Association Division
U.S. Chamber
of Commerce
Washington, D.C.**

Testifying

with Impact

By
Arch Lustberg

A "how to" booklet for those who testify on the federal, state or local levels of government.

Testifying with Impact
Original Edition 1982

1-9 copies.................................. $8.00 each
10-99 copies............................... $7.00 each
100 or more copies .... $6.00 each

Make check or money order payable to
Chamber of Commerce of the United States,
1615 H Street, N.W., Washington, D.C. 20062.

Contents

Preface

Executives who testify should give a high priority to learning the essential skills. If testimony is important enough to be delivered, it should be delivered with style—with IMPACT.

Testifying with Impact is an authoritative summary of the *do's* and *don't's* of effectively delivering testimony. It's "must" reading for association executives, business executives, counsel—in short, all people who might be called upon to testify on behalf of their organizations at all levels of government. It's also helpful to anyone who might have the opportunity to testify, whether before a congressional committee or the local school board.

We are indebted to Arch Lustberg, director of media education at the U.S. Chamber, for writing this important book.

Testifying with Impact is a useful guide and valuable reference. We urge you to read it, use it and bring it to the attention of your staff and colleagues.

Hugh McCahey
Manager
Association Division

Part

**Prologue:
Creating the
Opportunity
to Inform
and Persuade**

You probably consider testifying as a time-consuming, often dull exercise that's only a small, insignificant part of your professional responsibilities. This attitude is undoubtedly reflected in the lack of enthusiasm with which you testify or prepare others to testify at local, state and federal legislative or regulatory hearings. You should actually give a higher priority to learning how to effectively deliver testimony. You should consider it a unique opportunity to grab the attention of your audience and create the opportunity to inform and persuade.

Only a few years ago, the words "to testify" probably would have reminded you of a drama-charged courtroom with a cowering witness undergoing the relentless questioning of the shrewd, self-assured lawyer, Perry Mason.

Today it's far more likely that you think of testifying as an appearance before a panel of government officials where you state the position of your association on proposed legislation or regulations. For you, as for thousands of Americans, testifying has become part of your job.

In fact, it's quite possible that testifying has become commonplace for you, to the extent that you're no longer making the most of those opportunities to sway listeners to your point of view. It happens all too frequently that people deliver testimony in a way that makes it quite clear they're simply fulfilling another of the many responsibilities of their job.

What a difference it makes when testimony is delivered in the hope that a certain point of view will prevail! When such an attitude is adopted, anyone who delivers testimony will be on the right track toward achieving the two-fold objective of testifying: *to inform* and *to persuade*.

Some members of almost any government panel will have their minds firmly made up before hearings are scheduled. Testimony will possibly *inform* them but it probably won't *persuade* them.

But there are other panel members—and usually other listeners—who feel they should consider all arguments before reaching a decision or who have "gut reactions" that the force of a strong argument can alter. You can inform *and* persuade these people with your testimony.

Generally speaking, persuasion requires an appeal not only to listeners' logic but also to their emotions. Often the heavier emphasis is on the emotional appeal. People are persuaded to crave things which they really don't need. They learn to *want* them even though they don't *need* them.

Throughout history, the great persuaders have become the rich, the powerful, the successful. Think how many great leaders the world may have missed because certain great minds communicated with written words that appealed primarily to logic rather than to emotion. The fact that they didn't *talk* their messages is not an indication that their messages weren't brilliant. Aristotle, Shakespeare, Shaw, Kirkegaard, Voltaire, Dante, and St. Thomas Aquinas were all men of indisputable intellectual and literary brilliance. But the *persuaders* were Jesus, Moses, Napoleon, Caesar, Alexander, Hitler, and Roosevelt. They became leaders because they were exceptionally effective in *communicating their ideas to the people who heard them speak.* They often appealed to *logic*—but always to *emotion*.

In the theatre world, some actors are so magnificent they can read the telephone directory and move the audience to laughter or to tears. That's considered the ultimate compliment. On the other hand, it's all too possible for poor actors to make a brilliant play seem as dull as the telephone directory. The same is true of witnesses delivering testimony. What you have to say is important, but how well you say it is even more important.

This booklet will cover the *how to's* of delivering testimony—to make you the most effective communicator you can be, whether you're testifying at the local, state, or federal level or whether you're testifying before legislators, regulators, or a board of inquiry.

By learning and abiding by these *do's* and *don't's*, you'll gradually overcome any apprehension you have about delivering testimony. Testifying will no longer be an ordeal of reading words that appear on the paper in front of you. Instead, you'll begin to think of it as a valuable opportunity to communicate thoughts, ideas, and knowledge.

That's the concept this booklet will stress: testifying is not merely *reading words*, it's *communicating ideas*.

Let's go back to the scene that's replaced your old "Perry Mason" notion of testifying and be more specific about it. It's likely you imagine a top-level executive who puts on his half-bifocals, gazes down at his prepared text, and drones through pages of testimony composed by a public relations aide and quickly glanced at by the executive on his way to the hearing. The committee he's facing has just heard three other monotone recitations and is going to have to sit through three more before the session is over. It's no wonder, then, that one member is reading the morning paper, another is assiduously studying his recently chipped thumbnail, and a third has cupped his hand to one side of his mouth so he can tell an assistant what he wants for lunch. As you read on, keep this image in mind—and resolve to destroy it every time you're at the witness table.

The author demonstrates how a dull presentation of testimony can stand in the way of effective communication.

Today, very few local, state or federal bills or regulations are enacted without hearings. But very few of the people who speak at those hearings have learned the skills of effectively delivering testimony. So the person who speaks his piece clearly and confidently—who's energetic, pleasant, and sincere, and who delivers his ideas with *IMPACT*—has a tremendous advantage over the word readers. He or she is a communicator, someone who's grabbed the attention of listeners and created the opportunity to inform *and* persuade them.

This booklet was written to help *you* become that person.

2

How can you testify with such impact that you're assured of informing and persuading your listeners? You must first master the basics of breathing and relaxation. The importance of mastering these basics can't be overemphasized. The uncomfortable, tense, frightened speaker is assured of losing the attention of his audience. On the other hand, the relaxed, self-assured speaker has an excellent chance of informing and persuading his listeners.

The 1977 best-seller, *The Book of Lists*, includes a category called "The Fourteen Worst Human Fears." The number one fear: speaking before a group. It's hard to believe, but more people have a greater fear of public speaking than of death, job loss, killer insect bites . . . you name it.

The strongest enemy of good communication is *fear*. Call it nervousness, tension, pressure, self-consciousness, whatever you want. It's your foe.

The next strongest enemy of good communication is lack of *skill*. But before you develop the skills, you need to develop a sense of well-being that will conquer your fear.

The only people who've completely conquered fear are those who've been successfully speaking in public on a regular basis. Even then, certain unusual situations frequently arise that lead to panic. Think of the actor winning an Oscar. His profession calls for him to be in front of people all the time. He suddenly hears the words, "The envelope, please." He hears his name called. He dissolves into unintelligibility, trembling, sweating, stammering. He gives off all kinds of distress signals. If it can happen to an actor in Hollywood, it can certainly happen at a government hearing.

Those of us who've attended a lot of civic hearings for zoning variances, sanitation services, tenant/landlord clashes, school budgets and the like, or state legislature hearings, or federal congressional and regulatory hearings, are used to seeing the prototype of the harried Oscar-winner. We see a person who looks unhappy to be where he is—a person who's concerned, unloved and unwanted. He's sweating from every pore, clearing his throat, wetting his lips with a darting, snake-like tongue, wishing he were anywhere else in the world. He talks in a monotone of dread with bursts of words spurting out in staccato, machine-gun fashion. If it were possible to have a frown in the voice, he most certainly would. Unfortunately, his discomfort is contagious. The listener prays, "Dear Lord, help this poor, unfortunate wretch and deliver me from this boredom." Then he turns off his attention button.

How do you conquer the flustered speech and poor impression created by tension? How do you gain the confidence to smile at your listeners, to delight them—not with suave, slick delivery but with an easy, comfortable, conversational manner? The late Vince Lombardi created a dynasty of successful football teams by teaching and stressing—and restressing—the basics: blocking and tackling. Good oral communication also stresses the basics: breathing and relaxation. You can't be relaxed if you breathe incorrectly. You can't breathe correctly if you're tense.

So, the first step in effective communication—the foremost step in conquering tension—is proper breathing. The well-trained professional athlete, stage actor, opera singer or musician demonstrates proper breathing techniques under stress and bears watching. If the method is correct,

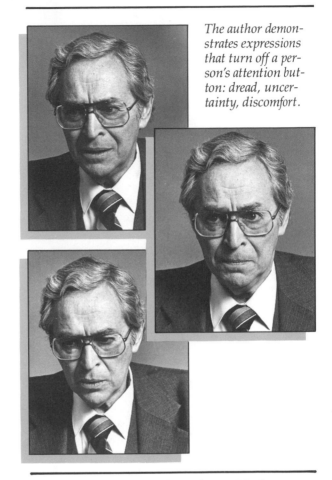

The author demonstrates expressions that turn off a person's attention button: dread, uncertainty, discomfort.

you won't notice the breathing. If it's wrong, you'll see the shoulders and upper chest move.

The best way to discover the correct breathing method is to lie down, close your eyes, place your fingers just under your rib cage (two to three inches above the navel), and concentrate on the rhythmic movement. On inhalation, the muscle under the fingers moves out. On exhalation, the muscle moves back in. The difficult part of this rhythm is that we've thought and been taught that inhalation means the muscle moves *inward* and that exhalation means the muscle moves *outward*.

The diaphragm is the muscle located just under the lungs. When the diaphragm flattens, it creates a greater space in which the lungs can fill. When the diaphragm returns, air is literally pushed out of the lungs.

Military and posture training have often resulted in poor breathing habits. We're told: "Head up, chin high, chest out, stomach in. Don't move that stomach!"

Breathing often becomes hindered by the effort to "hold in" the stomach. The diaphragm is not allowed to move *out* to make a correct rhythm. So much posture and military training have actually hurt our notion of correct breathing.

Once again, the key is to place the fingers just under the rib cage and force the fingers out—away from the body on the inhalation. The fingers should move back *toward* the body on the exhalation. Practice this rhythm. If you use the telephone a lot, a good time to continue this practice is when the cradle is in one hand at your ear. The fingers of the free hand should be placed under the rib cage. The movement should be controlled and noted.

If you've been doing it wrong for years, you can't correct it overnight. It requires effort—conscious effort. But the rewards are great. Proper breathing creates an almost instant feeling of well-being. You'll find you can immediately banish tension and stress as you're driving in very heavy, irritating traffic. The idiot ahead has just changed lanes and cut in front of you. Only a very fast reaction on your part avoided a collision. Take a few conscious, correct, deep breaths and notice how much better you feel. When you're livid with anger over some unnecessary stupidity at the office, try a few breaths and "watch" yourself relax, unwind.

The well-trained, well-coached athlete will do the same thing. Imagine: The basketball game is officially over. The tying goal was scored as the buzzer sounded. The player was fouled in the act of shooting. He must make one foul shot to win the game. The official tosses him the ball. He bounces it and "jiggles" every muscle in his body. He is all motion as he unwinds physically. He sets himself and takes a deep, imperceptible breath to unwind psychologically—to *create calm*. Then, he shoots. If you see his shoulders heave, he's breathing incorrectly.

Notice how many television newscasters, weather forecasters and sportscasters breathe incorrectly. You often see and hear their inhalations. *You shouldn't notice the big breath anywhere above the rib cage.* Good athletic coaches and good speech teachers will never ignore this step. In fact, the earlier it comes in the training, the faster the improvement and progress.

The second step in the war against tension is to learn *relaxation*. Breathing exercises certainly are a strong first step toward overcoming fear. Certain tension, stress or panic reducers are also invaluable in gaining a feeling of total confidence. The best way to relieve tension under pressure is to tighten the muscles, then relax them. We often succumb to tension because we're unaware of it. We know we're nervous, but we don't realize how much the muscles— especially of the head, neck and upper torso—have tightened.

The best, most complete exercise for reducing pressure is to stand and tense the toes. Drill them into the floor through the soles of your shoes. Tighten the calves. Move the tension up the thighs into the hips. *Don't let up.* Now tense your fingers.

Then tense your forearms. Move the tightness up the arms into the chest and down into the stomach. *Don't let up.* Tighten the muscles of the head and neck. Your body should be shaking from tension as you raise your arms over your head and stretch as far as you can. Now, relax. Drop the arms. Loosen all those muscles you've just subjected to extreme tension. Feel the surge of well-being that overtakes the entire body. The blood seems to flow naturally again to all parts of the body. The whole process should take under ten seconds. In that time, you'll know nearly complete tension followed by nearly complete relaxation—all of it superimposed and controlled by *you*.

Since you can't stand up and perform this exercise at a hearing, you should take any part of it and inconspicuously tighten and loosen the facial muscles while waiting to testify. You can even make yourself aware, while on the platform, that a tightness has attacked your head and neck muscles (the most common form of speech-making tension). By becoming aware of the tension, you can make these muscles relax.

A good way for you to achieve control is to practice tensing and relaxing your neck and head muscles. You can do this by drawing the neck taut until you can feel your vertical muscle and vein lines. Purse the lips and draw the jaw as tight as possible while clenching the teeth. Tighten the forehead until your eyes are barely open. Your entire head should be shaking. Now relax. This is the feeling you want to be able to recreate when nervousness, self-consciousness and fear seem to be turning into panic. You *can* control it. And if you do, your voice will be clear instead of wavering. Your saliva will flow more normally. You won't need to wet your lips incessantly as you talk. You'll experience a feeling of well-

The author demonstrates three practice steps for tensing and relaxing: 1. Draw the neck taut. 2. Purse the lips and draw the jaw tight while clenching your teeth. 3. Tighten your forehead until your eyes barely open.

being and *control* under pressure that you may never have felt before.

The combination of breathing and relaxation exercises is the best basic training experience for anyone about to face a tension-producing situation. For people who truly dread the experience of speaking in front of a group, the practice is invaluable.

We all know people who've *refused* to speak at a school board hearing because of *fear*. They're intelligent people who have strong views about the education of their children and the other children in the community. Yet, fear keeps their potentially persuasive views from being spoken. It shouldn't happen. It certainly doesn't have to happen. Nonetheless, it most definitely does happen.

Most executives don't suffer to the same degree. But any evidence of fear does get in the way of good communication.

So, breathing and relaxation are the basics of oral communication, and they deserve to be worked on even by those of us who consider ourselves reasonably good communicators.

Remember, the trained opera singer practices breathing and relaxation as assiduously as scales. They are the *basics*. Without them, the singer is less certain to hit the right note. The actor awaiting a cue in the wings will probably be concentrating on breathing and relaxation exercises. The athlete, as we mentioned earlier, does his exercises in front of the thousands in the grandstands and the millions on television. It really works.

Part

2

After you master the proper breathing and relaxation techniques, you should tailor the text, delivery, and style of your testimony to fit your own personality. It should be simple, crisp, sharp, conversational and natural. The end result should be like a conversation between you and someone you like very much.

Here are some ideas for you to consider so you'll give legislators and their staffs what they want when you testify:

First: Simplify the Text

Take the writer's language and convert it into your own. Use easy-to-understand words. Spiro Agnew's writers made him a laughing stock by using such words as *obfuscation* and *effete*. These and a host of other words and phrases fell poorly on the ear. Spoken transcript often makes rotten literature, and fine literary prose frequently *sounds* terrible when spoken.

Consider John F. Kennedy's inaugural address. It contained some truly lofty and brilliant prose that proved moving and emotionally stirring to millions of Americans. But it's almost impossible for the average person to read aloud. Consider:

> *Let the word go forth from this time and place, to friend and foe alike, that the torch has been passed to a new generation of Americans, born in this century, tempered by war, disciplined by a hard and bitter peace, proud of our ancient heritage, and unwilling to witness or permit the slow undoing of those human rights to which this nation has always been committed, and to which we are committed today at home and around the world.*

That's one sentence containing 80 words and seven commas. It's certainly not written in a style you would consider for testifying. It was designed for an inaugural address and for posterity.

From the same speech, another example of good literature but poor speechmaking—for anyone *but* the President—is this sentence:

> *Now the trumpet summons us again—not as a call to bear arms, though arms we need; not as a call to battle, though embattled we are; but a call to bear the burden of a long twilight struggle, year in and year out, rejoicing in hope, patient in tribulation, a struggle against the common enemies of man: tyranny, poverty, disease and war itself.*

That's 64 words, one dash, eight commas, two semi-colons and one colon.

Such rhetoric as *"though arms we need"* and *"though embattled we are"* just won't work for you and the average person when testifying before a committee. It doesn't work for most politicians either. Most of them haven't learned that lesson yet even though voters today seem to elect people who have mastered the technique of *talking* to their audience as opposed to *making a speech*.

A speech with simple language is easier to comprehend. The audience that *stops* to think about definitions, syntax and metaphorical imagery loses the next thought. (I'm not suggesting that a good speaker can't draw mental pictures. I *am* suggesting that these mental pictures must communicate instantly, or else you should make a reasonable pause to allow the digestion of the thought.)

Remove the jargon. Talk honest-to-goodness, understandable English. Governmentese, legalese, alphabetese, acronyms, catch words, and insider language (terms of the trade) should be totally eliminated from your text. I'll never forget a conversation I had with an army sergeant. When I asked him what his job was, he told me "I'm the N.C.O.I.C. for P.I.O. and I. and E. for the M.D.W." When later translated into English, I found out he was the Non-Commissioned Officer in Charge of Public Information, Troop Information & Education for the Military District of Washington.

Another example of how *not* to communicate is in the typical government bulletin style. Try this Internal Revenue Code information. It sounds like a comedian's parody, but it's the real thing:

> *For purposes of subsection (a)(l), a corporation shall not be considered to be a collapsible corporation with respect to any sale or exchange of stock of the corporation by a shareholder . . . if the shareholder owns more than 20 percent in value of the outstanding stock of the corporation and owns, or at any time during the preceding 3-year period owned, more than 20 percent in value of the outstanding stock of any other corporation more than 70 percent in value of the assets of which are, or were at any time during which such shareholder owned during such 3-year period more than 20 percent in value of the outstanding stock.*
> *. . . This paragraph shall not apply to any sale or exchange of stock to the issuing corporation or, in the case of a shareholder who owns more than 20 percent in value of the outstanding stock of the corporation, to any sale or exchange of stock by such shareholder to any person related to him (within the meaning of paragraph (8)).*

Wow! Over half the material was deleted by our editors, and it's still an endless mass of unintelligible words and phrases. If you skimmed or skipped it, no one would blame you. Not one simple, clear statement is made. And, incredibly, the bulk of it is one sentence.

Another point worthy of noting here is that nothing turns an audience off quite so quickly as use of pedantic, professional-sounding—but meaningless—terminology. Words like *parameters, interface, arcane* and *replicate* have become commonplace among jargon-spouting semantic dilettantes (that's the pot calling the kettle black) who intend to impress—but bore instead.

Use contractions. The apostrophe is one of the talker's best friends. *Don't, can't, let's, we'll, isn't, we're,* and most other contractions fall much more naturally on the ear than their equivalent two-word forms. In your preliminary planning, make one trip through your text with the exclusive purpose of converting every appropriate two-worder into a contraction. As a communicator, you'll find the apostrophe can be one of your strongest weapons. You'll see why when we talk about the presentation of testimony.

Make the speech your own. Go through the text idea by idea. Put everything into your own words. Just as important, put the thoughts into *your own sequence.* Your idea of continuity and structure will probably differ from the writer's. Make it as easy as possible for you to *talk* the text.

Punctuate in thought groups. In order to be conversational, the rhythm of your text should be idea by idea rather than word by word, phrase by phrase, or word group by word group. Many speakers use a stiff rhythm—pausing every two or three words. In formal speaking, that isn't their usual conversational rhythm. For example, former President Jimmy Carter used to break a sentence like this: "I think . . . we should . . . try to have . . . a better . . . understanding . . . of the forces . . . that make . . . our economy . . . inflationary." There's no reason for eight pauses in that 18-word sentence. Poor platform performance habits cause many speakers to demonstrate those rhythmic quirks. Maybe a lingering fear of running out of breath at the wrong moment is responsible. It would be far more effective for a speaker to take no pauses rather than eight. Or, if one is needed, it should be taken after the word *understanding*.

Second: Simplify the Delivery

It sounds so simple to say "talk, don't read," "chat, don't orate." But very few of us have acquired the skill of speaking one-on-one to a large group. When most executives approach the hearing room, they tend to clear the throat, place the voice back too far, tighten the facial muscles, and "look professional." It's really an unpleasant acting job. It certainly isn't the *real* person. Instead, it's the characterization we believe will impress our peers, and, certainly, most of our role models have led us down that road.

One of my favorite examples of doing what we *think* is expected rather than doing the *right* thing is this: Picture the police officer talking to his partner in the station house. "I caught this guy with the stolen television set," he tells his colleague. As he steps out of headquarters, the reporter and camera crew await him, throwing him into a totally unnatural environment (not unlike that of a hearing room). He clears his throat, buttons his jacket, "ahems" a few times and says, "We apprehended the alleged perpetrator leaving the crime scene with an appliance and no receipt." It's hard to believe, but most of us change our style in front of a group.

Every piece of testimony should be delivered as though it's a *conversation* between you and someone you like very much. You're not reading, you're explaining. Remember that the audience doesn't know what you know. You're there because you have something to say. Don't teach it, preach it, recite it, read it or orate it. *Say it. Tell it. Explain it.*

Remember how effective two- and three-word sentences can be. In fact, these are the sentences an audience remembers:

I love you.	*It's gorgeous.*
It's a boy.	*I knew it.*
She won.	*No one survived.*
They're dead.	*Wow!*
It burned.	*Certainly.*
It's ruined.	

Third: Select the Presentation Method That Suits You

Use the presentation form that suits you best. Some people are most effective using a prepared text. Some do their best work speaking from notes or an outline. Still others have a remarkable facility for delivering a talk from memory. Usually the message in a piece of testimony is so vital that *a manuscript is essential for complete accuracy.* Most witnesses feel more comfortable with a copy of the text in front of them. If you choose the prepared manuscript, remember not to use it as a crutch. Practice the delivery so your eyes aren't buried in your paper. The delivery techniques and preparation methods are the subject of the next chapter.

Part

4

Presentation: Sharpening Your Speaking Skills

You should become aware of certain speaking skills that will give added impact to your testimony. These skills are designed to make testimony conversational, clear, direct, pleasant, interesting and sincere. A final pointer that is often neglected is: "Prepare." You shouldn't testify unless you have fully prepared for every possibility. You should know your material so well that you can talk it and make it come alive.

In Part 2, you learned that fear is your number one enemy, with lack of proper skills close behind. You've learned some ways to control the tension, self-consciousness, pressure and stress that used to cripple you on the platform.

In Part 3, you learned some tips for writing statements that are effective when they're *heard* by others. You've learned to make the text, delivery and style a part of your own personality—a natural extension of yourself.

Part 4 is intended to help you achieve effectiveness in delivering testimony through an awareness and a sharpening of your speaking skills.

Let's consider some of the speaking skills and techniques that will help you achieve peak effectiveness. These skills will enable you to overcome many years of bad platform speaking habits that come from a lack of training and an overwhelming self-awareness.

The first step toward peak effectiveness is recognizing that all good oral communication is rooted in conversation. Even when you're watching an actor play Hamlet, he must make you feel as though he's *talking* to the people around him, and that in the soliloquies he's talking to you.

The second step is keeping in mind that communication is the transfer of ideas from one mind to another. Anything that interferes with the smooth, easy, effortless flow of an idea confuses or even destroys the communication.

When you're reading a book and see a gravy stain or a hair on the page, communication is interrupted. When a speaker has an unusual voice—a high-pitched, nasal, strained, hoarse sound, for example—communication is interrupted. A strange use of hands—such as a constant, rhythmic buttoning and unbuttoning of a jacket—can *destroy* communication.

If the interruption occurs while you're reading a book, you can go back and reread the page. Not so when the interruption comes during spoken communication. The damage can be irreparable. Effective oral communication depends on *clarity on the first try*.

There's a theory: If everyone could be successful as an oral communicator, we'd have no need for effective listening courses. The listener's mind usually wanders only when he's hearing an ineffective, less-than-dynamic talker. The talker must do everything possible to ensure smooth communication of ideas.

The third step toward peak effectiveness is being aware that every oral communication—except telephone, radio and recordings—involves the speaker's face and body as well as his voice. It's particularly important to remember that the hands and the face are NAKED . . . and they're usually the parts of the body we try to "hide" from the audience. Later in this chapter you'll get an idea of how awareness and control of what you do in animated conversation can help you look better, as well as sound better, as a witness.

The fourth step in achieving maximum effectiveness in oral communication is recognizing that the speaker should be pleasant and interesting to see and hear, should communicate logical meaning and attitude easily and directly, and should come across to an audience as a sincere person with a genuine desire to communicate these ideas. All very easy to say—but very difficult to accomplish. Let's see if we can make it easier and more natural for you.

The speaker should be pleasant and interesting to see.

The author demonstrates that fake jovial or insincere pleasant expressions alone are ineffective.

Being pleasant *or* interesting isn't enough.
The combination of the two is most effective.

A grin is pleasant. A smile is pleasant.
If neither is varied, the effect is studied,
dull, permanent, phoney.

A grotesque look may be interesting,
but it's hardly going to conquer audiences.

Here are a few illustrations that show
what speakers unknowingly do with their
faces, hands and bodies. Some expressions
can turn an audience off. Some can make
the audience concentrate on the *ideas* being
communicated.

*The author demon-
strates some of the
mannerisms which
distract from the
overall effect of the
testimony.*

The author demonstrates some of the mannerisms which distract from the overall effect of the testimony.

On certain occasions you may be one of several people testifying as a panel. When someone else is speaking, give that person your total attention—*physically* as well as *mentally*.

If you aren't aware of where you're looking, it can seem as though you don't care. And if you don't care, why should the listener?

The speaker should be pleasant and interesting to hear.

A soft, boudoir-sexy voice is pleasant enough. After five minutes without variation, it will put an audience to sleep. A grating, rasping voice is certainly interesting. It's also painful.

The person who . . . uh, uh . . . has a hard time . . . uh . . . uh . . . getting out . . . uh . . . the next . . . uh, uh . . . word . . . uh . . . without . . . uh . . . uh . . . making a sound (I call it the audible pause) is interesting but terribly irritating. Our urge is to help the unfortunate soul get the next word . . . uh . . . uh . . . uh . . . uh . . . OUT.

Return to the breathing exercises of Part 2. Place your hand on the area just below the rib cage. Take a few comfortable, relaxed breaths. On an exhalation, vocalize the sound "oo" (as in "to") quietly for about three seconds. Do it again in as low a pitch as possible. Now do it in as high a pitch as possible. Now do it with a middle, comfortable pitch. This sound, if your body is relaxed, will be the most pleasant, most interesting *BASIC* sound you can make without special coaching. Make this sound the one you use when delivering your testimony.

The speaker should communicate logical meaning and attitude easily and directly.

Every word, every phrase, every sentence makes some logical communication unless the entire receiving mechanism has been turned off out of total boredom or through some extraneous listening circumstance (a sudden severe stomach cramp hits the listener, an ambulance siren catches the hearer's *total* attention).

Every idea worth communicating contains an attitude, an emotion, a feeling. (If it doesn't, I urge you to edit the idea out of your testimony.)

Take the sentence, *"I thought Congress would pass the bill."* Logically, that says *"There was a piece of legislation proposed and I expected Congress to okay it."* The words alone say nothing, *zero*, about what actually happened. So, if it *did* pass, I'd speak those words in a very specific way. If it *didn't*, I'd speak those words in a totally different way. And, if that *totally stupid alternative bill passed* in its place, I'd have an entirely different delivery.

Try each aloud:

1. "I *thought* Congress would pass the bill." (And it did.)
2. "I thought Congress would *pass* the bill." (But it didn't.)
3. "I thought Congress would pass the *bill*." (But, would you believe it, those idiots *passed a rotten alternative*.)

You can probably think of more examples, but these three should help you understand that *what* you say can never convey complete meaning by itself. Listeners must also hear *HOW YOU SAY IT* to understand the total idea. That *HOW* is governed by three basic vocal tools that give you the techniques of creating emphasis to vary your sound. These tools are *volume*, *pitch* and *rate*.

- *Volume* is the decibel level of sound—the degree of loudness or softness.
- *Pitch* is the position of sound on the musical scale—the highness or lowness.
- *Rate* is the duration of sound—the fastness or slowness.

Volume variety is the least valuable, least effective vocal tool available to the speaker. It's great when the object is to discipline a child or an animal, or to wake a dozing audience, but that's rare. *"NO!"* shouted firmly and forcefully tells the youngster that what is being done is wrong and that he should "stop it." The most common use of volume in the wrong place is the politician who is either unskilled in platform speaking or running scared. The microphone and the audience are ignored as the politician shouts. Loud sounds are irritating, especially when the loudness is unabated and unnecessary.

The vocal variation of conversation is most often a combination of pitch and rate change. "How did you like it?" is the question. The reply is, "It was fantastic." If the word *fantastic* sounds like the two words preceding it, there is no emphasis and therefore no real meaning.

    FAAAAN
     TAS
     TIC is one way of saying it.

    FAAAAN
     TAAAAS
     TIC is another.

There are others, too. But the point is that the word deserves a pitch change and a rate change to make it mean what you want it to mean. In conversation, in gossip, in storytelling, in confidences, in mystery—rate as well as pitch is constantly changing for effect.

TRY:

```
              LIEEEEV     A
          BE                  B
1)   UNNNNN                     L
                                  E
```

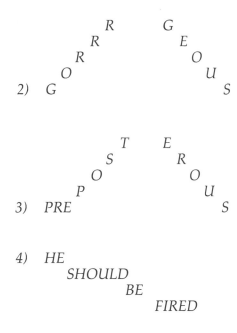

2) G O R R R G E O U S

3) PRE P O S T E R O U S

4) HE
   SHOULD
        BE
          FIRED

You can utter sounds and form words. But to really communicate, you must *express* yourself—and the best expression is uninhibited and unself-conscious.

1. I had a wonderful time.
   (Unless you do something wonderful with the word "wonderful," your host will think you're lying.)
2. It was a magnificent day.
   (Make *magnificent* truly magnificent.)
3. That garbage gave off the foulest smell.
   (It couldn't have been worse!)
4. Give me that knife.
   (If you don't, I'll shoot you.)

Very little of *that* kind of variation will happen at the hearing unless you make it happen. You've got to be willing to *exaggerate* in order to really make it come out the way you intended.

The author demonstrates correct, animated expressions that say "communicate."

That's vocal flexibility: the willingness and ability to use the vocal tools of pitch and rate.

There's also body flexibility. When you are seated at a witness table, body flexibility is a willingness and ability to lean forward and gesture in a natural manner when making a certain emphasis. Most of us "talk with our hands." That is, we tend to gesture in comfortable conversation. That tool—gesture—is a wonderful way of saying "I really want to get this point across to you." It's true communication.

We also tend to forget *facial* flexibility when the situation is formal. Most people are truly amazed when they see themselves on a television playback—amazed at how expressionless their faces are. They thought they were expressive. But that element of fear or self-consciousness caused them to duck back inside themselves rather than come out of themselves. Even natural extroverts tend to "pull in" when a stressful situation occurs.

The most vivid way to show the importance of this facial difference is through illustrations. When used correctly, the eyes are open, the brow is elevated, and the expression says "communication." When used incorrectly, the brows are drawn tight, the face is "closed," and the overly serious demeanor suggests "severe" if not "pompous ass". Unfortunately, the tendency is to look like the second example when we try to be professional, serious and business-like. We tend to dehumanize ourselves. In animated conversation, we more often look like the first example. It takes practice.

The speaker should come across as a sincere person with a genuine desire to communicate these ideas.

Quite often, we're forced to face a speaking situation under terrible circumstances. Testimony is scheduled for nine in the morning. We've been awake all night. The flu bug has bitten and we're miserable. The alarm goes off at 6:30, and it's not going to be a good day. Fortunately, the violent activity is over. But the pain and discomfort linger.

There's really only one thing to do: proceed.

It takes a lot of doing, but by concentrating, a *good job can be done* and the personal discomfort minimized. When the dis-

The author shows how discomfort can get in the way of communication.

comfort is allowed to take over, the legislators or regulators you're talking to may feel sorry for you; they may be kind and seem attentive. But you won't be communicating what you want. They'll receive signals of your discomfort rather than your ideas.

The techniques of looking and sounding interested must be used. Vocal and facial animation are essential. You've got to let gestures help make the voice and the face move. "Nothing is more important to me than getting these ideas across to you," is what you must say in attitude and expressiveness. Concentrate on *that*, not your personal problem.

One of the most important tools for impact is proper eye contact. It isn't just a matter of looking at the audience. Rather, it's looking at them at exactly the *right* moments. Usually, the beginning and the end of a sentence are *key* points for looking at a listener. Naturally, in order to do this and not to be totally dependent on the page, you've got to be familiar enough with your text to feel comfortable leaving the page.

The author shows how eye contact and expressions can work for and against you.

Most important, you've got to be willing to pause at the end of a thought—look down in *silence*, get your next idea in silence, look up and *then* begin speaking again.

These illustrations will show you how effective eye contact will give you greater impact.

To summarize, the person who testifies badly usually removes the papers from his case, puts on half bifocals, looks down at the pages and drones—reading words from page to page.

To help you achieve really effective eye contact, here are a few suggestions for preparing your testimony:

- Separate your pages. Remove clips and staples.
- Use large type.
- Double-space.
- Triple-space between paragraphs.
- Leave a *very* wide left-hand margin.
- Slide pages from right to left.
- Number pages in upper right-hand corner. (This will make the page number the first thing your eyes see as the new page is exposed.)
- Leave a two-inch margin at the bottom of the page. (Your head won't have to tilt down so far to see your bottom line.)
- Don't carry a sentence over to a new page. (Even if you lose another inch at the bottom of your page, don't start a new sentence.)
- Use the wide left-hand margin to give yourself guides. A sketch at the upper left-hand corner that looks like a smile can be a great help to remind you to look pleasant. If the speaker before you makes a point that reinforces yours, pencil in a marginal note referring to him.

Finally, in order to *present*, you must *prepare*. There should never be a time when you allow yourself to appear before legislators, regulators—or any audience for that matter—without going over and over the material. Writing a good piece of testimony or having it written for you isn't sufficient. You must make the ideas your own so that the material is delivered with your eyes mostly on the audience, not on the paper. Talk the message to the listeners, don't read it to them.

5

*You'll want to remember several miscella-
neous pointers when giving testimony. They're
really basics that every organized witness will
cover. They include remembering the mission,
knowing what's expected, concentrating totally on
persuasion, among others.*

First: Remember Your Mission

• **Concentrate on your audience.**
They're the reason you're testifying. It's important to realize exactly *who* is listening to
you. You have four audiences at most hearings:

1. Members of the body holding the
   hearings.
2. The press.
3. Staff.
4. Others (interested persons and
   those waiting to testify).

The committee members and the press
are the most important—and many of them
aren't knowledegable about your field. It's
vital to remember that fact. Even if they do
know something about your area of exper-
tise, chances are they didn't wake up this
morning concerned in any way with your
subject. The spokesperson for the metals
industry has to realize that the committee
members aren't thinking at their breakfast
table about supplies and prices of lead,
zinc, tin and copper. So don't get technical.
Simplicity and brevity are your stongest
tools. When in doubt, reread the Lord's
Prayer and the Gettysburg Address. Does it
surprise you to know that the Lord's Prayer
contains 56 words, the Gettysburg Address
326, the Declaration of Independence 1322
and a 1970s federal regulation on the sale of

red cabbage 29,611? (We confess we didn't do the counting ourselves.)

● **Come prepared with two texts—one detailed, one abbreviated.** Very often, the committee's chairperson will interrupt the witness after a few sentences:

"Sir (Madam), since our time is limited, please summarize your remarks for us."

There you are with your fourteen-page manuscript barely begun. You're totally unprepared for what happened. My suggestion—and it's been strongly endorsed by every legislator, regulator and staffer I've talked to—is to submit the full written testimony (with a copy at hand) and deliver the *briefest possible summary*. You'll score tremendous psychological points when, after the conclusion of the protocol and introductory remarks, you'll say:

"My entire statement was submitted to you, but now I'd like to give you a very brief summary of the text."

They *like* you for being considerate. They may even be impressed enough to go back and read your full text. It's more than a ploy; it's a courtesy. More often than not, you'll be rewarded with attention. You'll get more mileage out of *"We've got to do it,"* than with *"It is incumbent upon us all—each and every one—to see to it that appropriate action is taken at every level of endeavor."* When in doubt, cut another third.

● **Get advice on your remarks from others who are expert.** Then completely convert their sequence, ideas and words into your own. If possible, try out your remarks on non-experts so you're sure the language and flow are easily understood. This way, you'll have a better chance to sound genuine and convincing, to draw empathy and understanding from an audience of strangers.

● **Learn everything you can in advance that's relevant about your audience.** It's very helpful to know the names and titles of the people you're addressing. And don't overlook the correct pronunciation. Nothing is more embarrassing than the wrong name or pronunciation. The old television series "Mission Impossible" began with a series of photos and biographical backgrounds on all the key people in each episode. It's not a bad idea for you, in the preliminary stages, to learn about the people who'll be listening to you. Of the four audiences mentioned earlier, the committee conducting the hearing is the one to whom you're talking and the one about whom you need to learn.

Second: Know What's Expected of You

● **Pay attention to protocol.** Be attentive to niceties, good taste and common sense. It's taken centuries to build up the convention of protocol. Don't try to destroy it single-handedly.

The conscientious witness thanks the panel for the opportunity to speak. The *good* witness *means* it. A good piece of testimony contains a brief self-introduction, unless a previous witness has done it. The good witness gives the personal details—as well as the entire testimony—with interest, animation and pride. He also should identify the bill that's the subject of the testimony, and his position.

Witnesses should be polite, but they shouldn't cave in under pressure. They shouldn't allow badgering by committee members.

● **Make your points concisely and coherently.** Good sense and good taste dictate that you state your conclusion first. The entire text should then flow logically to again reach that conclusion at the end. Repeat your key points in different ways. If possible, use examples that will relate to specific people on the panel: to their pocketbooks, to their families, and to the pocketbooks and families of their constituents. It's no secret that certain federal regulations regarding air bags and other automotive safety devices will add considerably to the purchase price of a new car. If safety is your message, no amount of money is too much to save a life. If cost is your concern, every new automobile will cost an additional $200 (or whatever the accurate figure is) for *everyone*, whether or not he wants the features. Remember that coherence is often fortified when you're colorful, quotable, memorable, delightful, newsworthy. Your effectiveness depends on the audience remembering you. Keep in mind the old show business adage: "Always leave them wanting more." If you succeed, it's possible they'll take another look at the full text to see if it contains even more useful information. Remember, the standard vaudeville act lasted 12 minutes. The *briefer* your testimony, the greater the impact.

● **Be positive.** Stay with your argument. It's perfectly good rhetoric to set up your opponent's case if you can demolish it with logic and wit. Generally, however, stay with the positive side of your case. Relate it to real people, not statistics. The statement: *"We've seen a 100 percent increase in the cost of a loaf of bread in the most recent five-year period"* isn't as effective as *"A loaf of bread cost you 30 cents to put on your table five years ago. Today, that same loaf of bread is smaller and costs 60 cents."* Make your presentation brief, clear, sympathetic, understandable, and *real-people* oriented. In that way, you'll find you get more mileage out of it.

Third: Remember Persuasion

Everyone in your audience falls into one of three ideological categories:

1. Those who are on your side—and you want to keep them there.
2. Those who oppose your views—and you'd like to convert them.
3. Those who haven't made up their minds.

The best strategy is to talk to those who haven't decided. It's unlikely that you'll change strongly held views. Some of your best weapons as a persuader are to:

- Know the issue—not just the general facts, but the details should be part of your mental filing cabinet.
- Know the other side. You're at your best when you have the opposition's information down as pat as they do. Nothing is as damaging psychologically as stammering and pausing audibly uh-uh-uh when delivering testimony or uh-uh-uh-answering-uh-uh-uh questions. It seems to be uncertainty, lack of confidence, and worse, lack of preparation. Conversely, nothing gives you greater credibility than the confidence that comes with complete knowledge of the opposition's argument and the ability to state your case more authoritatively and convincingly than they do.
- Know the bill or regulation under consideration. If possible, know it at least as well as the people conducting the hearings. Take the time to receive a thorough briefing from the most knowledgeable experts available. Nothing can replace complete knowledge combined with assured

delivery. There should be no sur-
prises—and no one will be able to
make you look bad for lack of information.

- Rehearse your presentation thor-
oughly—until you're totally comfortable with it. Then have staff, associ-
ates and other experts you trust put
you through the kind of questioning
you're most likely to face by the most
hostile panelists. If you can handle
the nasties, you can do well with the
friendly questions.

Fourth: Things Your Testimony Should Be

- Simple.
- Brief. Don't try to tell them all you know.
- Expert.
- Well-organized.
- Well-documented.
- Logical.
- Persuasive.
- First-class argumentation.
- Colorful. Use real examples about real
people.
- Quotable.
- Well-constructed; wonderfully delivered.
- Positive.
- Submitted at least 48 hours in advance of
your scheduled appearance.
- Neat.

And Finally

Every piece of testimony should con-
tain certain basic information:

- Identification of Individuals Appearing
—Name, title, affiliation.
—Background to establish credibility as a
witness.
—Identity of organization and constitu-
ency you're representing.

- Identification of Legislation or Issue
  —Specify bill by number, issue by title.
  —State your position briefly and early.
  —Paraphrase and colloquialize your understanding of the intent or purpose of the legislation or issue.
- Areas under Consideration
  —Define them.
  —If supportive, explain why.
  —If opposed, state why and give alternatives if any exist.
- Statement of Your Position and Your Argument
- Summation including What You'd Like to See Accomplished

Your spoken testimony can have far greater impact than your written submission. Spoken words have greater life, color, vividness and excitement. If you do *really* well, someone may want to go back and read your entire text.

Letters and written texts may get lost in the sheer volume of paperwork. Your material may reach one staffer whose bias or workload prevents him from giving it the attention it deserves. It's a little like the phone book: they only find what they're looking for.

So, once again, remember to submit the entire testimony in writing and then orally present an extremely shortened, very lively version. Brilliantly delivered, it will win the day.

Part 6

Particulars:
A List of
Do's and Don't's

I t's hoped you've learned from this booklet that your testimony is a tightly knit composite of content and delivery. Each is important. Most association executives have very little or no problem with the material. The delivery is the common stumbling block. So, as a final note, here are some *do's* and *don't's* that summarize the techniques stressed in this booklet. Look down this list before *every* appearance until you feel truly comfortable about testifying.

DO	*DON'T*
Communicate ideas.	Read words.
Be interesting.	Be dull.
Consider appearance an opportunity.	Consider appearance a chore.
Be energetic.	Be dull, lifeless.
Be pleasant.	Be intimidated.
Grab the audience.	Put listeners to sleep.
Make your audience pleased to be listening to you.	Make your audience wish it were somewhere else.
PRACTICE breathing and relaxation exercises.	*IGNORE* the importance of breathing & relaxation.
Move your diaphragm *OUT* on inhalation.	Pull your diaphragm *IN* on inhalation.
Move your diaphragm *IN* on exhalation.	Push your diaphragm *OUT* on exhalation.
Learn to relax throughout tense moments.	Get tense and *stay* that way.

Smile when appropriate.	Frown.
Communicate attitude and feeling.	Rely purely on logical content.
Vary pitch and rate.	Use more volume than you need to be heard.
Gesture for emphasis.	Tie up your hands *or* wave into the air.
Open up your face.	Tighten your facial muscles.
Say what you mean *and* mean what you say.	Recite words from a page.
Prepare.	Trust yourself to luck.
Use vocal and facial exercises.	Assume you'll be animated under stress.
Interest your audience.	Bore.
Concentrate on the *material*.	Think about yourself.
Talk, chat or converse an oral summary.	Read, preach, orate a long, detailed, wordy piece of testimony.

About the Author

Arch Lustberg, who is director of media education at the Chamber of Commerce of the United States, is known throughout the association community for his popular Communicator® Workshops, designed to train executives to meet today's many communication challenges.

A former faculty member of the Speech and Drama Department of the Catholic University of America in Washington, D.C., he has privately coached members of Congress, the Cabinet and network broadcasters.

In addition to teaching and coaching, he produced and directed *Gallant Men*, the award-winning record album of Senator Everett M. Dirksen, and *The Voice of the People*, the U.S. Capitol Historical Society album narrated by Helen Hayes and E.G. Marshall.

He also produced the Broadway musical, *Don't Bother Me, I Can't Cope*.

Federal Tax Treatment of Unrelated Business Income
Order #5555 $3.50 each

From trade shows to T-shirts . . . from magazine ads to mailing lists, a growing number of associations are selling products and services that provide the revenue needed to fund new programs or simply to offset the effects of a slow economy. This publication outlines the legislative and judicial history of federal tax treatment of unrelated business income.

Financial Management Handbook
Order #3106 $5 each

A comprehensive look at the financial organization and policies of associations: budgeting, functional accounting, account classification, cost control, unrelated income, cash flow, investments, financial statements and more. Written by a major accounting firm's non-profit organization specialists in conjunction with a task force of association executives.

Association Committees
Order #5342 $4 each

A booklet for association executives and members who want committees to play an important role in overall association operations. Includes general information on organization, make-up and activities.

Association Bylaws
Order #5446 $3.50 each

A booklet of sample association bylaws—most followed by explanations of specific provisions and comments on their purposes and common variations. Drawn from actual bylaws of a wide range of established, successful associations.

Guidelines for An Association Seeking a Chief Staff Executive
Order #6060 $3 each

Practical advice on how to locate, evaluate and hire the best available person to head an association staff—compiled from ideas and suggestions of top association executives experienced in selection procedures.

Associations and the Antitrust Laws
Order #5152 $8 each

The book tells how association programs and practices that are susceptible to antitrust violations can be kept within the law as well as how to establish evidence of compliance in the event of an antitrust charge. Pricing activities, statistical programs, certification, product standards and other areas of antitrust exposure are discussed.

Associations and the Law Series (5 volumes)
Order #6109 $27 per set

The set includes 74 articles on the legal requirements and ramifications of association activities. Each article—written by an experienced attorney—covers a single legal matter in concise, non-technical language. Subjects include association taxation, legislative and political action; antitrust laws; government regulation; certification and credentialing; insurance programs and labor law.

Understanding Agency Procedures: Administrative Law
Order #5714 $8 each

A basic explanation of how your organization can play a key role in government agency decision-making. It tells when, where and how to state your position on regulations before they're enacted.

The Federal Dragnet
Order #5726 $3.50 each

An overview of federal investigative processes that tells how investigations can be directed at your association and how to best protect your association's legitimate interests and personal rights during such an investigation.

Legislators and Regulators Appraise Associations
Order #5494 $2 each

This pamphlet summarizes survey results of state and federal legislators and regulators on the effectiveness of association government relations activities. Subjects include services most valuable to government officials and steps to take in developing a more effective government relations program.

Associations and Lobbying
Order #6137 $9 each

This book discusses tax aspects of lobbying by trade and professional associations as well as by charitable and educational groups; antitrust implications of association lobbying and effects of the 1976 Tax Reform Act on public charities. Appendices include texts and official interpretations of relevant laws and regulations, a list of court decisions regarding lobbying and suggested reference materials.

Dialogue with Government Officials
Order #6376 $2.50 each
This book gives observations of congressional and federal agency staff members on how association executives can communicate effectively with government legislative and administrative bodies.

Government Relations Reference Materials
Order #5138 $2 each

An alphabetical listing of 41 widely respected government affairs publications, periodicals and general reference volumes.

Testifying with Impact
Order #6560 $8 each

When you testify, you get one chance. No re-takes. No repeats. This book shows you how to communicate effectively when testifying on the federal, state or local levels of government.

An Order Form for these publications is on the following page!

Publications for Associations

Association executives will want to keep the Chamber's complete association reference library close at hand.

Order your copies by returning this Order Form.

ASSOCIATION MANAGEMENT AND OPERATIONS	Unit Price	Quantity	Total Price
Federal Tax Treatment of Unrelated Business Income (#5555)	$3.50		$
Financial Management Handbook (#3106)	5.00		
Association Committees (#5342)	4.00		
Association Bylaws (#5446)	3.50		
Guidelines for An Assn Seeking a Chief Staff Exec (#6060)	3.00		

ASSOCIATIONS AND THE LAW			
Associations and the Antitrust Laws (#5152)	8.00		
Associations and the Law Series, Books V-IX (#6109)	27.00		
Associations and the Law, Book V (#3160)	7.00		
Associations and the Law, Book VI (#3982)	7.00		
Associations and the Law, Book VII (#5397)	7.00		
Associations and the Law, Book VIII (#5605)	7.00		
Associations and the Law, Book IX (#6099)	8.00		

ASSOCIATIONS AND GOVERNMENT			
Understanding Agency Procedures: Administrative Law (#5714)	8.00		
The Federal Dragnet (#5726)	3.50		
Legislators and Regulators Appraise Associations (#5494)	2.00		
Associations and Lobbying Regulation (#6137)	9.00		
Dialogue with Government Officials (#6376)	2.50		
Government Relations Reference Materials (#5138)	2.00		
Testifying with Impact (#6560)	8.00		

ORDER FORM

Send me the publications checked above.

☐ Bill me.   ☐ Check enclosed (payable to U.S. Chamber); California and District of Columbia residents add sales tax.

Name

Organization

Address

City/State/Zip

Mail to: Hugh McCahey, U.S. Chamber of Commerce, 1615 H Street, N.W., Washington, D.C. 20062